Purpose of Life

Tawanda Tawanda

Published by Tawanda Tawanda, 2024.

Also by Tawanda Tawanda

Life After Divorce
African Child
Purpose of Life

The purpose of life is not to be found in what we achieve, but in who we become in Christ. Our true fulfillment is found in aligning our hearts with God's will, and living with the eternal perspective He has given us.

Disclaimer:

The information and ideas presented in Purpose of Life are intended for informational and inspirational purposes only. While the author has made every effort to ensure the accuracy of the material presented, the author makes no representations or warranties regarding the completeness or accuracy of the content, nor does the author assume any liability for any errors or omissions.

The views expressed in this book are those of the author and do not necessarily reflect the opinions or beliefs of any organization, religious group, or other entity. The book's content is not intended to serve as professional or legal advice. Readers are encouraged to seek appropriate guidance and counseling where necessary.

By reading this book, the reader acknowledges and agrees to the terms of this disclaimer. The author is not responsible for any loss, injury, or damages arising from the use or application of the information contained within.

Dedication

I dedicate this book to my spiritual father and mother, L. Mangwiro, with deep gratitude for the invaluable lessons you have taught me, the prayers you have offered on my behalf, and the wisdom you continue to share. Your guidance has been a beacon of light in my life. May the Lord bless you richly for all that you have imparted into my life.

— Tawanda Tawanda

Chapter 1: Introduction – The Quest for Purpose

What is the purpose of life? This timeless question stirs within every human heart, prompting reflection, curiosity, and a search for deeper meaning. Whether in moments of triumph or tragedy, solitude or celebration, we are drawn to contemplate the significance of our existence. Why are we here? What is our role in the grand story of creation?

The Bible offers a profound insight into this question in Ecclesiastes 3:11, which says: "He has made everything beautiful in its time. He has also set eternity in the human heart; yet no one can fathom what God has done from beginning to end." This verse reveals a divine truth about humanity: we are created with a longing for eternity, a spiritual awareness that this life is not all there is.

The Universal Longing for Meaning

From the dawn of time, humanity has sought answers to life's most pressing questions. Ancient philosophers pondered the meaning of existence, while modern thinkers explore purpose through science, art, and psychology. Despite differing perspectives, one thing remains constant: the human heart is restless until it finds something greater than itself.

King Solomon, one of the wisest men to ever live, explored this restlessness in his own life. As he chronicled in the book of Ecclesiastes, he pursued wealth, wisdom, pleasure, and achievements—only to find that none of these could truly satisfy. His conclusion? Life without God is like "chasing the wind."

This longing for meaning is universal because it originates from the One who created us. God placed eternity within our hearts, giving us an intrinsic awareness that we are part of something far greater than our earthly existence. However, this awareness also comes with a challenge: we cannot fully comprehend God's eternal plan on our own. This tension drives our quest for purpose, leading us to seek answers in various ways—some fruitful, others fleeting.

Purpose as a Journey

Life's purpose is not a single destination but a journey. It is discovered gradually, unfolding as we walk through different seasons and experiences. In this journey, we face moments of joy and sorrow, certainty and doubt, all of which shape our understanding of who we are and why we exist.

At the heart of this journey lies a relationship with God. The Bible teaches that our ultimate purpose is rooted in Him:

To know Him (John 17:3: "Now this is eternal life: that they know you, the only true God, and Jesus Christ, whom you have sent.")

To glorify Him (Isaiah 43:7: "Everyone who is called by my name, whom I created for my glory, whom I formed and made.")

To reflect His love and truth to the world (Matthew 22:37-39).

Life's meaning is not confined to a specific career, achievement, or role. It is about living in alignment with God's will, seeking Him daily, and allowing His Spirit to guide us.

An Invitation to Seek

The quest for purpose is an invitation to walk closely with God, trusting Him to reveal His plan for our lives. This journey is personal and transformative, but it is not without challenges. Along the way, we encounter distractions, setbacks, and questions that test our faith. Yet, as we draw near to God, He draws near to us (James 4:8).

In the chapters ahead, we will explore what it means to live with purpose in every season of life. From the joy of discovering God's plan to navigating loneliness and pain, each step offers an opportunity to grow closer to Him.

As you read, let Ecclesiastes 3:11 serve as a guiding light: "He has set eternity in the human heart." This eternal perspective reminds us that our purpose is far greater than anything this world can offer. It is found in knowing and walking with the One who created us for His glory.

The journey of purpose begins with a simple yet profound step: seeking God. Are you ready to embark on it?

Chapter 2: Created for a Purpose

From the beginning of time, humanity's existence has been marked by a profound truth: we are not accidents, nor are we the result of random chance. We were created by a loving and intentional God, designed with care and purpose. This foundational truth is beautifully captured in Genesis 1:27:

"So God created mankind in his own image, in the image of God he created them; male and female he created them."

This verse reveals a central aspect of our identity: we are made in the image of God. But what does it mean to be created in God's image, and how does this connect to our purpose?

—-

The Image of God

Being made in God's image, or Imago Dei, is a concept that distinguishes humanity from all other creations. Unlike animals or plants, we are spiritual beings with the capacity to reason, love, create, and relate to God. This divine imprint gives every human life intrinsic value and a calling to reflect God's character.

Reflecting God's image means we are called to mirror His attributes, such as love, justice, mercy, creativity, and holiness. In this way, our purpose is not just about what we do but about who we are. We glorify God by embodying His character in our daily lives.

—-

Purpose Tied to God's Character

Our purpose as God's image-bearers is inherently tied to our relationship with Him. We were not only created by God but for God. Colossians 1:16 affirms this: "All things have been created through Him and for Him." This means our ultimate purpose is to glorify God and live in fellowship with Him.

1. To Glorify God

To glorify God is to reflect His greatness and honor Him in all we do. This happens when we live in alignment with His will, using our gifts, talents, and resources for His glory. Jesus emphasized this in Matthew 5:16: "Let your light shine before others, that they may see your good deeds and glorify your Father in heaven."

When we love, serve, and live with integrity, we reflect God's character to the world. This is not about perfection but about living as vessels through which His light shines.

2. To Enjoy Him Forever

God desires a relationship with us, not just obedience or service. The Westminster Catechism states: "The chief end of man is to glorify God and enjoy Him forever." This enjoyment comes from knowing God deeply, walking with Him daily, and experiencing the peace and joy that only He can provide.

Psalm 16:11 captures this beautifully: "You make known to me the path of life; you will fill me with joy in your presence, with eternal pleasures at your right hand." Our purpose is not burdensome but a source of fulfillment and delight when rooted in God.

—-

Living with Purpose as Image-Bearers

Understanding that we are created in God's image shapes how we view ourselves, others, and the world around us.

1. Self-Worth and Identity

Knowing that we are made in God's image gives us a sense of worth that is not dependent on achievements, possessions, or societal standards. We are valuable simply because God created us and loves us. This truth is a powerful antidote to insecurity and self-doubt.

2. How We Treat Others

Every human being, regardless of race, gender, or status, bears God's image. This means we are called to treat others with dignity, respect, and compassion. Jesus summarized this in the command to love our neighbors as ourselves (Matthew 22:39).

3. Our Role in Creation

As image-bearers, we are also entrusted with stewardship of God's creation. Genesis 1:28 describes how God gave humanity the responsibility to "fill the earth and subdue it." This involves caring for the environment, nurturing relationships, and contributing to the flourishing of the world around us.

—-

The Fulfillment of Purpose in Christ

While humanity was created to reflect God's image, sin distorted this purpose. Our selfishness, pride, and rebellion against God marred the reflection of His character in our lives. However, God's love for us never wavered. Through Jesus Christ, we are restored to our original purpose.

Jesus, the perfect image of God (Colossians 1:15), came to reconcile us to the Father. Through His life, death, and resurrection, we are given the opportunity to live out our purpose as redeemed image-bearers. As we grow in Christlikeness, we increasingly reflect God's glory and fulfill our calling.

—-

A Life of Glorifying and Enjoying God

To live with purpose is to embrace our identity as God's image-bearers, created to glorify Him and enjoy Him forever. This purpose is not limited to specific careers, roles, or achievements. Whether we are students, professionals, parents, or friends, our purpose is fulfilled in the way we live as reflections of God's character.

In the words of the apostle Paul: "So whether you eat or drink or whatever you do, do it all for the glory of God" (1 Corinthians 10:31).

As we move forward, let us remember that our worth, identity, and purpose are rooted in the One who created us. We are not aimless wanderers but beloved children of God, made for His glory and eternal joy.

Chapter 3: The Joy of Living

Life's journey, though marked by challenges and uncertainties, is meant to be lived with joy. This joy is not a fleeting emotion dependent on favorable circumstances but a deep, abiding sense of peace and contentment found in God. It is a gift, a fruit of the Spirit that grows within us as we walk in step with Him.

Galatians 5:22 teaches us: "But the fruit of the Spirit is love, joy, peace, forbearance, kindness, goodness, faithfulness, gentleness, and self-control." Joy, as one of these fruits, reflects the work of the Holy Spirit in our lives. It is not something we manufacture ourselves but something God produces within us when we abide in Him.

—-

Joy Beyond Circumstances

The world often defines joy as happiness tied to external factors—success, wealth, relationships, or accomplishments. However, the Bible reveals a different kind of joy, one that is independent of life's highs and lows.

The apostle Paul, writing from a prison cell, declared in Philippians 4:4: "Rejoice in the Lord always. I will say it again: Rejoice!" His circumstances were far from ideal, yet his heart overflowed with joy because it was rooted in Christ, not in his surroundings.

This kind of joy comes from:

1. A Relationship with Christ: True joy begins with knowing Jesus as Lord and Savior. Through Him, we experience forgiveness, reconciliation with God, and the promise of eternal life. John 15:11 says,

"I have told you this so that my joy may be in you and that your joy may be complete."

2. Trust in God's Sovereignty: Joy flourishes when we trust that God is in control and His plans are good, even when life is difficult. Romans 8:28 reminds us, "And we know that in all things God works for the good of those who love him, who have been called according to his purpose."

3. Hope in Eternity: When we view life through the lens of eternity, our struggles lose their power to rob us of joy. We are reminded that this life is temporary and that eternal joy awaits us in God's presence (Psalm 16:11).

—-

Cultivating Joy in Daily Life

While joy is a gift from God, it also requires intentional effort to nurture and cultivate. Here are practical ways to grow in joy:

1. Gratitude

Gratitude shifts our focus from what we lack to what we have, opening our hearts to the blessings of God. When we practice gratitude, we acknowledge God's goodness and faithfulness, even in difficult times.

Practical Steps: Keep a gratitude journal, listing three things you're thankful for each day. Take time in prayer to thank God for His blessings, both big and small.

2. Service

Serving others brings joy because it reflects the heart of Christ. Jesus Himself said, "It is more blessed to give than to receive" (Acts 20:35). When we serve, we experience the fulfillment of being God's hands and feet in the world.

Practical Steps: Volunteer at a local charity, help a neighbor in need, or simply offer encouragement to someone going through a tough time.

3. Worship

Worship draws us into God's presence, where true joy is found. Psalm 100:2 invites us: "Worship the Lord with gladness; come before him with joyful songs." In worship, we shift our focus from our problems to the greatness of God, allowing His joy to fill our hearts.

Practical Steps: Spend time in personal worship, sing songs of praise, and join a community of believers to celebrate God's goodness.

—-

Joy in Trials

One of the most remarkable aspects of biblical joy is its ability to endure through trials. James 1:2-3 challenges us: "Consider it pure joy, my brothers and sisters, whenever you face trials of many kinds, because you know that the testing of your faith produces perseverance."

Trials, though painful, have a purpose. They refine our faith, deepen our dependence on God, and remind us of His sustaining power. When we choose to trust Him in the midst of hardship, we discover a joy that the world cannot take away.

—-

Living Out the Joy of Christ

The joy of living is not about avoiding difficulties or chasing temporary pleasures. It is about embracing the life God has given us, trusting in His plan, and walking in relationship with Him.

As we grow in gratitude, serve others selflessly, and worship God with all our hearts, we experience a joy that transcends circumstances. This joy becomes a testimony to the world, a reflection of the hope we have in Christ.

In the words of Nehemiah 8:10: "The joy of the Lord is your strength." May this joy sustain you, strengthen you, and lead you to live with purpose and passion every day.

Chapter 4: The Weight of Sadness

Life is not without its shadows. As much as we desire joy, sorrow is an unavoidable part of the human experience. Loss, disappointment, betrayal, and suffering remind us of the brokenness of our world. Yet, in the midst of sadness, there is purpose. The Bible teaches that sorrow, though painful, can refine us, deepen our dependence on God, and draw us closer to His heart.

Psalm 34:18 offers a comforting truth: "The Lord is close to the brokenhearted and saves those who are crushed in spirit." In our moments of deepest sorrow, God's presence is near, offering solace and strength.

—-

Sorrow as Part of the Human Experience

Sadness is not foreign to Scripture. The Bible is filled with raw expressions of grief and lament, showing us that sorrow is not a sign of weakness or lack of faith. Instead, it is part of what it means to be human in a fallen world.

1. Job: A Man of Unimaginable Loss

The story of Job is one of the most poignant examples of human suffering. In a single day, Job lost his children, wealth, and health. His friends offered shallow explanations for his pain, but Job remained honest in his lament, crying out to God with questions and anguish.

Yet, in his sorrow, Job's faith endured. He declared: "The Lord gave and the Lord has taken away; may the name of the Lord be praised" (Job 1:21). Job's story reminds us that even in our darkest moments, God is sovereign and faithful.

2. David in the Psalms

David, the "man after God's own heart," often poured out his sadness in the Psalms. His words resonate with anyone who has experienced despair:

"My tears have been my food day and night" (Psalm 42:3).

"Why, my soul, are you downcast? Why so disturbed within me?" (Psalm 42:11).

Yet, even in his sorrow, David consistently turned to God, affirming his trust in His promises:

"The Lord is my rock, my fortress and my deliverer" (Psalm 18:2).

David's example teaches us that we can bring our pain to God honestly, trusting Him to be our refuge.

—-

The Comfort of God's Promises

In times of sadness, God's promises become a source of hope and strength. The Bible assures us that God is not distant or indifferent to our pain.

1. God is Near

Psalm 34:18 reminds us that "The Lord is close to the brokenhearted." God's presence is most tangible when we are hurting. He draws near to comfort, heal, and restore.

2. God Understands Our Pain

Through Jesus, God Himself entered into human suffering. Isaiah 53:3 describes Jesus as "a man of sorrows, acquainted with grief." He understands our pain because He endured it Himself.

3. God's Promises of Restoration

The Bible assures us that sorrow will not last forever. Revelation 21:4 offers a vision of hope: "He will wipe every tear from their eyes. There will be no more death or mourning or crying or pain, for the old order of things has passed away."

—-

How Sadness Refines Us

While sadness is painful, it also has a refining purpose.

1. It Deepens Our Faith

In times of sorrow, we are reminded of our dependence on God. When everything else feels uncertain, His unchanging nature becomes our anchor. As Paul writes in 2 Corinthians 12:9: "My grace is sufficient for you, for my power is made perfect in weakness."

2. It Cultivates Compassion

Experiencing sadness helps us empathize with others. As we are comforted by God, we are equipped to comfort those around us (2 Corinthians 1:4).

3. It Purifies Our Hearts

Sorrow has a way of stripping away superficial concerns, redirecting our focus to what truly matters. Psalm 119:71 says, "It was good for me to be afflicted so that I might learn your decrees." In sadness, we often grow in wisdom and spiritual maturity.

—

Drawing Closer to God in Sorrow

Sadness, while heavy, is an invitation to draw closer to God. Here are practical ways to find Him in the midst of sorrow:

1. Pour Out Your Heart

God invites us to bring our pain to Him. Like David in the Psalms, we can pray honestly, expressing our grief without fear of judgment.

2. Seek His Word

Scripture is a source of comfort and hope. Passages like Psalm 23 and Isaiah 41:10 remind us of God's presence and faithfulness in difficult times.

3. Lean on the Church

God often works through His people to bring comfort and support. Sharing your burdens with trusted friends, pastors, or small groups can be a source of strength.

4. Rest in His Presence

In times of sadness, quiet moments in prayer and worship allow us to feel God's peace. As Jesus said in Matthew 11:28: "Come to me, all you who are weary and burdened, and I will give you rest."

—

The Purpose in Pain

While sadness is never easy, it is not meaningless. God uses sorrow to shape us, deepen our relationship with Him, and prepare us for the joy of eternity. As Romans 8:18 reminds us: "I consider that our present sufferings are not worth comparing with the glory that will be revealed in us."

The weight of sadness may press on us, but it also lifts our eyes to God, the source of true comfort and hope. In His presence, we find healing, restoration, and the promise of eternal joy.

Chapter 5: The Loneliness of the Journey

Loneliness is a deeply human experience. It whispers to us in moments of isolation, reminding us of our vulnerability and need for connection. At times, even when surrounded by others, we may feel unseen or misunderstood. The Bible does not shy away from this reality. Many of its great figures, including Elijah, David, and even Jesus, faced seasons of profound loneliness.

Yet, even in our loneliness, we are never truly alone. God's promise in Deuteronomy 31:8 is a balm for the soul: "The Lord Himself goes before you and will be with you; He will never leave you nor forsake you. Do not be afraid; do not be discouraged."

This chapter explores the loneliness we encounter on life's journey and how it can be transformed into a season of spiritual growth and deeper intimacy with God.

—-

Loneliness in the Bible

Loneliness is not new; it is a shared challenge across generations. The Bible records stories of individuals who endured isolation, yet found God's presence to be their greatest comfort.

1. Elijah: Loneliness in the Wilderness

After a victorious showdown with the prophets of Baal, Elijah fled into the wilderness, overwhelmed with fear and exhaustion. Feeling utterly alone, he cried out to God: "I have had enough, Lord. Take my life" (1 Kings 19:4).

In his solitude, God met Elijah—not with rebuke, but with gentle care. He provided food, rest, and, eventually, a still, small voice that reminded Elijah of His presence (1 Kings 19:12). Elijah's story teaches us that God sees us in our loneliness and ministers to us tenderly in our darkest moments.

2. Jesus: The Loneliness of the Cross

Jesus, too, experienced profound loneliness. In the Garden of Gethsemane, He prayed in anguish, while His closest friends slept (Matthew 26:36–46). On the cross, He cried out: "My God, my God, why have you forsaken me?" (Matthew 27:46).

Jesus' loneliness was not just physical but spiritual, as He bore the weight of humanity's sin. Yet, through His isolation, He accomplished the ultimate act of love, reconciling us to God. His experience assures us that He understands our loneliness and walks with us through it.

—-

God's Promise in Loneliness

In our moments of loneliness, it is easy to feel abandoned. Yet, Scripture reminds us that God is always with us:

Deuteronomy 31:8: "The Lord Himself goes before you and will be with you; He will never leave you nor forsake you."

Psalm 23:4: "Even though I walk through the darkest valley, I will fear no evil, for You are with me."

Isaiah 41:10: "Do not fear, for I am with you; do not be dismayed, for I am your God."

These promises reveal that God's presence is not contingent on our feelings. Even when we cannot sense Him, He is there, guiding and sustaining us.

—-

The Purpose of Solitude

While loneliness can be painful, it can also serve a purpose in our spiritual journey. Times of solitude often become opportunities for growth and transformation.

1. Solitude as a Time of Reflection

In the noise of daily life, it can be difficult to hear God's voice. Solitude provides a space to reflect, pray, and seek His guidance. Jesus Himself often withdrew to lonely places to pray (Luke 5:16).

Practical Steps: Use moments of loneliness to journal your thoughts, meditate on Scripture, and ask God to reveal His purpose for this season.

2. Solitude as a Time of Preparation

Many of God's greatest servants were shaped in isolation. Joseph spent years in prison, Moses tended sheep in the desert, and Paul endured time alone in Arabia before beginning his ministry. These seasons were not wasted; they were times of preparation for the work God had for them.

Encouragement: Trust that God is working in your solitude, preparing you for the next chapter of your journey.

3. Solitude as a Time of Intimacy with God

In loneliness, we often turn to God with a vulnerability we might not otherwise have. Psalm 46:10 invites us: "Be still, and know that I am God." It is in the stillness of solitude that we come to know God more deeply.

—-

Overcoming the Pain of Loneliness

While loneliness can have a purpose, it is not something we are meant to bear alone. God provides ways to overcome its sting:

1. Seek Community

God designed us for relationship. While there are times of necessary solitude, we are also called to live in fellowship with others. Hebrews 10:24–25 encourages us: "Let us consider how we may spur one another on toward love and good deeds, not giving up meeting together."

Practical Steps: Join a small group, reach out to a friend, or become involved in your church community.

2. Serve Others

Loneliness often tempts us to turn inward, but serving others shifts our focus outward. Acts of kindness not only bless others but also bring fulfillment and connection.

Practical Steps: Volunteer at a local organization or offer support to someone who may also be feeling isolated.

3. Cling to God's Word

Scripture is a source of comfort and strength. Memorizing verses about God's presence can anchor you in truth during lonely times.

—-

Loneliness and the Purpose of Life

The loneliness of the journey reminds us that we were created for relationship—first and foremost with God. In our isolation, we recognize our need for Him and discover that He is more than enough.

Ultimately, loneliness points us to the eternal truth that we are never truly alone. As Jesus promised in Matthew 28:20: "Surely I am with you always, to the very end of the age." Let this promise be a light in the dark, guiding you toward the One who walks with you every step of the way.

Chapter 6: What Am I Living For?

Every human heart longs to answer a profound question: What am I living for? The search for purpose drives our ambitions, relationships, and choices. Yet, the Bible offers a clear and transformative answer. Jesus Himself summarized life's ultimate purpose in Matthew 22:37–39:

"Love the Lord your God with all your heart and with all your soul and with all your mind. This is the first and greatest commandment. And the second is like it: Love your neighbor as yourself."

In these verses, we find that the purpose of life is twofold: to love God and to love others. These are not separate goals but deeply intertwined pursuits. When we align our hearts with these commands, we discover the meaning and fulfillment we were created for.

—-

Loving God: The Foundation of Life's Purpose

Our primary purpose is to love God wholeheartedly. This love is not merely a feeling but a commitment to prioritize Him in every aspect of life.

1. What Does It Mean to Love God?

Loving God means seeking Him above all else. It means living in a way that glorifies Him and reflects His character. Jesus said in John 14:15: "If you love me, keep my commands." Love for God is expressed through obedience, worship, and devotion.

2. How Do We Cultivate Love for God?

Spend Time with Him: Just as relationships grow through time and communication, our love for God deepens when we spend time in prayer, worship, and Scripture.

Reflect on His Love: 1 John 4:19 reminds us: "We love because He first loved us." When we meditate on God's sacrificial love through Jesus, our hearts respond with gratitude and love.

Surrender Fully: To love God with all our heart, soul, and mind requires surrendering our plans, desires, and fears to Him, trusting that His will is perfect.

Loving God is not just an obligation; it is the source of true joy and fulfillment. Psalm 16:11 declares: "You make known to me the path of life; You will fill me with joy in Your presence, with eternal pleasures at Your right hand."

—-

Loving Others: The Overflow of Loving God

The second part of our purpose is to love others as ourselves. This command is inseparable from the first. When we love God, His love flows through us to those around us.

1. Who Are We Called to Love?

Our Neighbors: This includes family, friends, colleagues, and even strangers. Loving our neighbors means showing kindness, compassion, and respect.

Our Enemies: Jesus challenges us to love not only those who are easy to love but also those who hurt or oppose us (Matthew 5:44). This radical love reflects the heart of God.

2. How Do We Love Others?

Serve: Loving others often involves serving them in practical ways. Galatians 5:13 encourages us: "Serve one another humbly in love."

Forgive: Love requires forgiveness. Just as God forgives us, we are called to extend grace to others (Ephesians 4:32).

Encourage: Words have the power to uplift and inspire. Hebrews 10:24–25 urges us to "spur one another on toward love and good deeds."

Loving others is not always easy, but it is always worthwhile. When we love selflessly, we reflect God's character and fulfill His purpose for our lives.

—-

Finding Purpose in Everyday Actions

Purpose is not limited to grand achievements or significant milestones. It is found in the ordinary moments of life when we live with faith and love.

1. Faith in the Ordinary

Colossians 3:23 reminds us: "Whatever you do, work at it with all your heart, as working for the Lord, not for human masters." Whether we are working, studying, or caring for our families, we can glorify God by doing our tasks with excellence and integrity.

2. Service in the Small Things

Simple acts of kindness—helping a neighbor, listening to a friend, or offering a word of encouragement—are profound expressions of love. As Jesus said in Matthew 25:40: "Whatever you did for one of the least of these brothers and sisters of mine, you did for me."

3. Witnessing Through Your Life

When we live with purpose, others notice. Our actions and attitudes can point people to God and inspire them to seek Him. Matthew 5:16 encourages us: "Let your light shine before others, that they may see your good deeds and glorify your Father in heaven."

—-

Aligning Personal Goals with God's Plan

God created each of us uniquely, with specific gifts, passions, and opportunities. While our ultimate purpose is to love God and others, our individual callings may look different.

1. Seek God's Guidance

Proverbs 3:5–6 advises: "Trust in the Lord with all your heart and lean not on your own understanding; in all your ways submit to Him, and He will make your paths straight." When we invite God into our decision-making, He aligns our goals with His plan.

2. Use Your Gifts for His Glory

1 Peter 4:10 teaches: "Each of you should use whatever gift you have received to serve others, as faithful stewards of God's grace in its various forms." Whether through teaching, creating, leading, or helping, we can use our talents to make an impact for God's kingdom.

3. Trust His Timing

Sometimes, our plans do not unfold as expected. In such moments, we can trust that God's timing is perfect and His purposes are greater than we can imagine (Isaiah 55:8–9).

—-

Living for God's Glory

Ultimately, the purpose of life is not about achieving personal success or happiness but about glorifying God. As the Westminster Catechism famously states: "The chief end of man is to glorify God and enjoy Him forever."

When we love God, love others, and align our daily actions with His will, we fulfill the purpose for which we were created. This is not a burdensome task but a life of freedom, joy, and meaning.

May our lives echo the words of Paul in Philippians 1:21: "For to me, to live is Christ and to die is gain." Let us live with purpose, knowing that every moment has eternal significance.

Chapter 7: Youth – The Energy of Beginnings

Youth is a season filled with energy, ambition, and potential. It's a time of exploration and discovery, when life feels like a blank canvas waiting to be painted with dreams and opportunities. However, it is also a critical period for laying a strong foundation—one that will support the rest of life's journey.

The Apostle Paul's words to Timothy in 1 Timothy 4:12 provide timeless encouragement: "Don't let anyone look down on you because you are young, but set an example for the believers in speech, in conduct, in love, in faith and in purity." This verse reminds us that youth is not a limitation but a unique opportunity to live boldly for Christ and make a difference.

—-

The Gift of Youth

1. Strength and Vitality

Youth is often marked by physical and mental strength. Ecclesiastes 12:1 urges: "Remember your Creator in the days of your youth, before the days of trouble come." The energy and resilience of youth are gifts meant to be invested wisely.

Practical Application: Use this season to explore your God-given talents, serve others with enthusiasm, and pursue goals that align with God's purposes.

2. The Freedom to Learn and Grow

Young people are not yet weighed down by many of life's responsibilities. This freedom provides a unique opportunity to learn, grow, and seek God wholeheartedly. Psalm 119:9 asks: "How can a young person stay on the path of purity?" The answer: "By living according to Your word."

Practical Application: Dedicate time to studying Scripture, building strong relationships, and developing habits that honor God.

—-

Building a Strong Foundation in Christ

Just as a house needs a solid foundation to stand firm, a life needs a spiritual foundation rooted in Christ.

1. The Importance of Early Faith

Faith established in youth often shapes the course of a person's life. Proverbs 22:6 teaches: "Start children off on the way they should go, and even when they are old they will not turn from it." Building a relationship with God early provides guidance and stability during life's challenges.

2. Spiritual Disciplines

Prayer: Develop a habit of daily prayer to stay connected to God.

Scripture: Study and memorize God's Word to strengthen your faith.

Community: Surround yourself with believers who can encourage and challenge you.

3. Overcoming Distractions

The world is full of distractions that can pull young people away from their purpose. Social media, peer pressure, and the pursuit of worldly success can cloud the path God has set. Matthew 6:33 reminds us: "Seek first His kingdom and His righteousness, and all these things will be given to you as well."

—-

Balancing Ambition with Humility

Youth is often accompanied by ambition—a desire to achieve and make a mark on the world. While ambition can be a powerful force for good, it must be balanced with humility and obedience to God.

1. Ambition Aligned with God's Will

James 4:15 advises: "Instead, you ought to say, 'If it is the Lord's will, we will live and do this or that.'" Ambition should not be about self-glorification but about glorifying God and serving others.

2. The Danger of Pride

Proverbs 16:18 warns: "Pride goes before destruction, a haughty spirit before a fall." While pursuing goals, it is essential to remain humble and acknowledge that all success comes from God.

3. Learning Obedience

Jesus Himself demonstrated the importance of obedience during His youth. Luke 2:51 records: "Then He went down to Nazareth with them and was obedient to them." If the Son of God valued obedience, how much more should we?

—-

Setting an Example as a Young Believer

Paul's exhortation in 1 Timothy 4:12 challenges young people to set an example in five areas:

1. Speech

Use words to build others up and glorify God. Ephesians 4:29 encourages: "Do not let any unwholesome talk come out of your mouths, but only what is helpful for building others up."

2. Conduct

Live a life that reflects Christ's character. Colossians 3:17 reminds: "Whatever you do, whether in word or deed, do it all in the name of the Lord Jesus."

3. Love

Show Christlike love to others, even when it is difficult. John 13:35 says: "By this everyone will know that you are my disciples, if you love one another."

4. Faith

Demonstrate unwavering trust in God, even when faced with challenges. Hebrews 11:6 declares: "Without faith it is impossible to please God."

5. Purity

Maintain moral integrity in thoughts, actions, and relationships. 1 Thessalonians 4:3 reminds: "It is God's will that you should be sanctified: that you should avoid sexual immorality."

—

Youth and the Purpose of Life

Youth is not just a time to prepare for the future but a season to live purposefully in the present. By loving God, serving others, and aligning ambitions with His will, young people can fulfill their God-given purpose even in their earliest years.

Practical Encouragement:

Pursue a relationship with God passionately.

Seek mentors who can guide you in your faith and decisions.

Dream big but hold those dreams with open hands, trusting God's plan above all.

As Ecclesiastes 12:13 concludes: "Fear God and keep His commandments, for this is the duty of all mankind." Let the energy and potential of youth be directed toward eternal purposes, building a life that glorifies God and impacts others.

Chapter 8: Maturity – The Beauty of Wisdom

Maturity is more than the passage of time; it is the deepening of character, understanding, and purpose. As we grow, life teaches us lessons that transform us from impulsive youth to wise stewards of God's truth. Proverbs 4:7 encourages us: "The beginning of wisdom is this: Get wisdom. Though it cost all you have, get understanding."

Wisdom is the hallmark of maturity, and it begins with recognizing that life is not about us but about glorifying God. As we journey through trials, triumphs, and transitions, we grow in wisdom and understanding, becoming reflections of Christ's character.

—-

The Process of Growing in Wisdom

Wisdom is not innate; it is cultivated through time, reflection, and a relationship with God.

1. The Fear of the Lord

Proverbs 9:10 teaches: "The fear of the Lord is the beginning of wisdom, and knowledge of the Holy One is understanding." True wisdom starts with reverence for God—acknowledging His sovereignty and submitting to His will.

Practical Application: Regularly seek God's guidance in prayer and through Scripture. Trust His ways even when they differ from your own understanding (Proverbs 3:5–6).

2. Learning from Experience

Life's experiences—both good and bad—are opportunities to grow in wisdom. Mature individuals learn from their mistakes and allow their experiences to shape their decisions.

Practical Application: Reflect on past experiences and ask God what lessons He wants you to learn. Journaling can be a helpful tool for capturing these insights.

3. Seeking Wise Counsel

Proverbs 15:22 reminds us: "Plans fail for lack of counsel, but with many advisers they succeed." Maturity involves humility—the willingness to learn from others.

Practical Application: Surround yourself with godly mentors and seek their advice in times of decision-making.

—-

Shifting from Self-Centered Goals to God-Centered Living

As we mature, our focus shifts from seeking personal gain to fulfilling God's purpose. This transformation requires us to let go of self-centered ambitions and embrace a life of service and obedience.

1. Recognizing God's Sovereignty

Maturity begins with the realization that our lives are not our own. 1 Corinthians 6:19–20 declares: "You are not your own; you were bought at a price. Therefore honor God with your bodies."

Practical Application: Reevaluate your goals and ask, "Do they align with God's will?"

2. Living for God's Glory

A mature believer lives to glorify God in every aspect of life—work, relationships, and service. Colossians 3:17 encourages: "Whatever you do, whether in word or deed, do it all in the name of the Lord Jesus."

Practical Application: Commit your daily actions to God. Even mundane tasks can become acts of worship when done with the right heart.

3. Serving Others

Philippians 2:3–4 urges: "Do nothing out of selfish ambition or vain conceit. Rather, in humility value others above yourselves, not looking to your own interests but each of you to the interests of the others." True maturity involves putting others' needs before your own, modeling Christ's selfless love.

—-

The Role of Trials in Producing Perseverance

Maturity is often forged in the crucible of trials. While challenges can be painful, they are also opportunities for growth. James 1:2–4 reminds us: "Consider it pure joy, my brothers and sisters, whenever you face trials of many kinds, because you know that the testing of your faith produces perseverance. Let perseverance finish its work so that you may be mature and complete, not lacking anything."

1. Trials as Refinement

Just as fire refines gold, trials refine our character and faith. They reveal areas of weakness, teach us dependence on God, and strengthen our perseverance.

Biblical Example: Joseph endured betrayal, slavery, and imprisonment before becoming a ruler in Egypt. His trials prepared him to fulfill God's purpose of saving many lives (Genesis 50:20).

2. Trusting God in Hard Times

Romans 8:28 assures us: "And we know that in all things God works for the good of those who love Him, who have been called according to His purpose." Maturity involves trusting that God's plans are good, even when we cannot see the outcome.

Practical Application: In moments of difficulty, remind yourself of God's promises and remain steadfast in prayer.

3. Perseverance Leads to Hope

Romans 5:3–5 explains: "We also glory in our sufferings, because we know that suffering produces perseverance; perseverance, character; and character, hope. And hope does not put us to shame." Trials deepen our hope in Christ, anchoring us in His faithfulness.

—-

The Beauty of Maturity

Maturity is not about perfection but about progress. It is the continual process of becoming more like Christ.

1. A Life of Contentment

Mature believers learn to find contentment in God, rather than in worldly achievements or possessions. Philippians 4:12–13 states: "I have learned the secret of being content in any and every situation... I can do all this through Him who gives me strength."

2. A Life of Influence

Maturity equips us to be examples for others. Titus 2:7 encourages: "In everything set them an example by doing what is good." A mature life inspires and guides others in their faith journey.

3. A Life of Eternal Perspective

Mature believers focus on what truly matters—eternity. Colossians 3:2 urges: "Set your minds on things above, not on earthly things." This perspective brings peace and purpose, even in the face of life's uncertainties.

—-

Embracing the Journey of Maturity

Maturity is not a destination but a lifelong journey. It requires patience, perseverance, and a willingness to grow. As we seek wisdom, shift our focus to God-centered living, and endure trials with faith, we become vessels of His grace and glory.

Let us echo the words of Paul in Philippians 3:14: "I press on toward the goal to win the prize for which God has called me heavenward in Christ Jesus." May the beauty of wisdom and the depth of maturity guide us as we fulfill our purpose in Him.

Chapter 9: The Role of Relationships

Human beings are inherently relational creatures, created to connect with one another and, ultimately, to reflect the love of God through these connections. Relationships are not just a byproduct of life—they are woven into the very fabric of our existence. From the beginning, God declared, "It is not good for the man to be alone" (Genesis 2:18), setting the foundation for the importance of relationships in our lives. Whether it's family, friendship, or community, our relationships are designed to shape us, refine us, and help us live out our purpose.

Jesus' command in John 15:12—*"My command is this: Love each other as I have loved you"—*summarizes the essence of life's relational purpose. Our relationships reflect God's love for us, and in turn, we are called to extend that love to others.

—-

Exploring Relationships as a Reflection of God's Love

At the heart of all relationships is the call to love. God's love for humanity is the ultimate example, and as we seek to live according to His purposes, we are invited to mirror that love in every interaction.

1. God's Love is Selfless and Sacrificial

In John 15:13, Jesus says: "Greater love has no one than this: to lay down one's life for one's friends." True love in relationships is selfless, choosing to serve the other person even at great personal cost. Christ demonstrated this love by laying down His life for us, and we are called to do the same.

Practical Application: In relationships, practice selflessness by putting others' needs before your own, seeking their well-being over personal gain.

2. God's Love is Unconditional

God's love is not dependent on our performance but is given freely, despite our imperfections. This unconditional love is the foundation for our relationships with others.

Practical Application: Cultivate unconditional love by forgiving others, even when it's difficult, and by embracing people as they are—flaws and all.

3. God's Love is Transformative

Love has the power to change hearts, heal wounds, and build unity. When we love others as Christ loves us, we reflect His transformative power.

Practical Application: Strive to be a conduit of God's transforming love in your relationships, seeking to bring peace, healing, and growth to those around you.

—-

The Importance of Community, Friendship, and Accountability

We were never meant to walk alone in this life. God designed us to thrive in community, where we are encouraged, challenged, and supported by others.

1. The Power of Christian Community

Acts 2:42–47 gives a beautiful picture of the early Church living in vibrant community: “They devoted themselves to the apostles' teaching and to fellowship, to the breaking of bread and to prayer.” Community is essential for growth, both spiritually and emotionally. In the context of a faith community, we can learn, serve, and hold one another accountable.

Practical Application: Actively engage in a church or small group where you can build relationships, grow in your faith, and serve others.

2. Friendship as a Gift

Proverbs 27:17 teaches: “As iron sharpens iron, so one person sharpens another.” Friendship is a vital aspect of our relational journey, offering a space for encouragement, laughter, and mutual growth. True friends challenge one another to become better versions of themselves, growing in character and faith.

Practical Application: Build deep, meaningful friendships that encourage spiritual growth. Be intentional about investing time and energy in these relationships.

3. The Necessity of Accountability

Accountability in relationships keeps us grounded and helps us stay on track with our purpose. Proverbs 27:5–6 says: “Better is open rebuke than hidden love. Wounds from a friend can be trusted, but an enemy multiplies kisses.” Accountability helps us recognize areas of weakness and encourages us to live in accordance with God's will.

Practical Application: Invite trusted friends or mentors to hold you accountable in your spiritual walk, finances, relationships, and personal growth. Be open to constructive feedback and correction.

—-

How Relationships Shape and Refine Us for God's Glory

God uses relationships to mold us into the people He desires us to be. Through our interactions with others, He teaches us lessons of love, humility, patience, and forgiveness.

1. Relationships Reveal Our Character

Relationships provide a mirror to our character. How we treat others—especially when they disappoint or hurt us—reveals our true nature. The Apostle Paul encourages us in Ephesians 4:2 to "Be completely humble and gentle; be patient, bearing with one another in love."

Practical Application: Use relationships as an opportunity to examine your own heart. Are you loving, patient, and humble? Do your actions reflect Christ's character?

2. God Refines Us Through Conflict

Conflict is inevitable in relationships, but it is also an opportunity for growth. James 1:2–4 reminds us that trials, including relational struggles, "produce perseverance; let perseverance finish its work so that you may be mature and complete."

Practical Application: When conflict arises, instead of avoiding it or reacting in anger, ask God to help you navigate it with wisdom and grace, seeking reconciliation and growth in the process.

3. God Uses Relationships to Grow Us in Humility

Serving others in relationships requires humility. Philippians 2:3–4 teaches us: "Do nothing out of selfish ambition or vain conceit. Rather, in humility value others above yourselves, not looking to your own interests but each of you to the interests of the others." God uses relationships to teach us to die to self and live for others.

Practical Application: Practice humility in your relationships by serving others, being quick to forgive, and not demanding your own way.

—-

The Eternal Perspective on Relationships

In the end, relationships are not merely about the present moment—they are an opportunity to reflect God's eternal love and to prepare for eternity. Jesus prayed in John 17:3: "Now this is eternal life: that they know you, the only true God, and Jesus Christ, whom you have sent." Relationships are a key part of God's plan, both for this life and the life to come.

1. Eternal Relationships in God's Kingdom

In heaven, relationships will be perfected—no more division, pain, or hurt. Revelation 21:4 promises: "He will wipe every tear from their eyes. There will be no more death or mourning or crying or pain, for the old order of things has passed away." Our relationships on earth are a foretaste of the perfect unity we will experience with God and one another for eternity.

2. Relationships as a Reflection of the Gospel

The way we love and care for others serves as a reflection of the gospel. Jesus said in John 13:35, "By this everyone will know that you are my disciples, if you love one another." Our relationships are a powerful witness to the world of God's love for humanity.

—-

Conclusion

Relationships are a key part of life's purpose. They reflect God's love, shape our character, and refine us for His glory. Through community, friendship, accountability, and even conflict, God uses relationships to help us become more like Christ. Let us embrace the role that relationships play in our journey, understanding that they are not just means of support but avenues through which we fulfill our purpose in God's grand plan.

May our relationships be a testimony of the love of Christ, drawing others to Him as we live in community with one another, bearing each other's burdens, and growing together in faith.

Chapter 10: The Battle with Self

The journey of life is not only a pursuit of purpose in relation to God and others but also an internal battle—a battle with ourselves. This internal struggle is one of the most difficult, as it involves our deepest desires, our pride, and the lingering effects of sin within us. Every day, we are confronted with choices that challenge us to either submit to the flesh or to yield to the Spirit. The battle with self is universal, for as long as we live in this world, we will wrestle with our sinful nature. However, it is through surrender to God and reliance on His grace that we can overcome.

—-

The Struggle Against Pride, Selfishness, and Sin

At the heart of the battle with self lies the struggle against pride, selfishness, and sin. Pride leads us to exalt ourselves above others and above God, while selfishness blinds us to the needs of others and seeks to fulfill our desires at the cost of relationships. Sin, in all its forms, is the root of our discontent and our separation from God.

1. Pride: The Root of Many Struggles

Pride is a fundamental aspect of our fallen nature. It was pride that led Lucifer to rebel against God, and it is pride that continues to disrupt our relationship with Him and with others. Proverbs 16:18 warns: "Pride goes before destruction, a haughty spirit before a fall."

Practical Application: Combat pride by embracing humility. Remember that everything you have and achieve is by God's grace. Seek to serve others rather than seeking to be served, as Jesus taught in Matthew 20:26-28.

2. Selfishness: The Desire to Fulfill Our Own Will

Selfishness is the tendency to focus solely on our own needs and desires, often to the detriment of others. It is the opposite of the self-sacrificial love that Jesus demonstrated. Philippians 2:3-4 urges us: "Do nothing out of selfish ambition or vain conceit. Rather, in humility value others above yourselves, not looking to your own interests but each of you to the interests of the others."

Practical Application: Break the chains of selfishness by practicing generosity—whether with time, resources, or kindness. Consider the needs of others and seek to serve them, just as Christ came to serve.

3. Sin: The Battle Within

Sin is a destructive force within every human being. Even after accepting Christ, we are not exempt from its influence. It is a constant temptation to go our own way, to follow desires that are contrary to God's will. Romans 7:18-19 expresses Paul's inner conflict: "For I have the desire to do what is good, but I cannot carry it out. For I do not do the good I want to do, but the evil I do not want to do—this I keep on doing."

Practical Application: Acknowledge that sin is real, but refuse to let it dominate your life. Be proactive in resisting temptation by immersing yourself in Scripture, prayer, and fellowship with believers.

—-

Biblical Insight: Paul's Inner Conflict (Romans 7:15-25)

Paul's struggle with sin provides a vivid picture of the battle within us all. In Romans 7:15-25, Paul describes the frustration of knowing what is right but failing to live according to it. He acknowledges the reality of sin's power, even in the life of a believer: "For I have the desire to do what is good, but I cannot carry it out" (Romans 7:18). Paul's internal conflict reveals that even the most faithful among us will face temptations and failures, but this doesn't mean we are defeated.

1. The Reality of Our Struggle

Paul's words give us insight into the deep frustration and despair that often accompany our battle with sin. We desire to please God, but our flesh constantly pulls us in the opposite direction. This struggle is universal—it is a part of the Christian experience. But Paul doesn't leave us in despair.

2. The Cry for Deliverance

In Romans 7:24, Paul cries out, "What a wretched man I am! Who will rescue me from this body that is subject to death?" This cry is not one of hopelessness but of desperation, longing for deliverance. It reflects the believer's yearning for freedom from sin's power and the longing for the redemption that only God can provide.

Practical Application: When you find yourself struggling with sin, call out to God for help. Remember that you are not alone in your battle, and He is always ready to rescue and restore you.

3. The Victory in Christ

In Romans 7:25, Paul offers a note of hope: "Thanks be to God, who delivers me through Jesus Christ our Lord!" While the struggle against sin is real, the victory has already been won through Christ. In Him, we find deliverance and the power to overcome our sinful nature. Through

Christ's sacrifice, we are no longer slaves to sin but are set free to live in righteousness.

—-

Overcoming Through Surrender to God and Reliance on His Grace

The key to overcoming the battle with self is surrender. We cannot fight the battle on our own strength, for we are weak in our own power. But God's grace is sufficient for us. In 2 Corinthians 12:9, Paul writes: "But he said to me, 'My grace is sufficient for you, for my power is made perfect in weakness.' Therefore I will boast all the more gladly of my weaknesses, so that the power of Christ may rest upon me."

1. Surrendering to God

Surrender is the act of yielding ourselves completely to God. It is a daily choice to place our will in His hands and to rely on His strength rather than our own. Jesus' example in the Garden of Gethsemane shows us the power of surrender: "Not my will, but Yours be done" (Luke 22:42).

Practical Application: Each day, commit your will to God in prayer. Ask Him to guide your thoughts, desires, and actions, and submit to His leadership in every area of your life.

2. Relying on God's Grace

Grace is God's unmerited favor, given freely to us despite our flaws and failures. It is through God's grace that we are empowered to resist temptation and live according to His will. Hebrews 4:16 encourages us: "Let us then approach God's throne of grace with confidence, so that we may receive mercy and find grace to help us in our time of need."

Practical Application: When you face temptation or struggle with sin, remember that God's grace is sufficient. Approach Him in humility, ask for His strength, and trust in His ability to help you overcome.

3. Living in the Power of the Holy Spirit

The Holy Spirit is our helper, given to us to guide, convict, and empower us to live godly lives. Romans 8:13 reminds us: "For if you live according to the flesh, you will die; but if by the Spirit you put to death the misdeeds of the body, you will live." It is by the power of the Holy Spirit that we can overcome the desires of the flesh and live in alignment with God's will.

Practical Application: Surrender to the Holy Spirit daily. Seek His guidance in moments of temptation, and trust that He will empower you to overcome.

—-

Conclusion: Victory Through Christ

The battle with self is real, but it is not one we fight alone. Through Christ, we have the power to overcome pride, selfishness, and sin. Our victory is found not in our own efforts but in surrendering to God, relying on His grace, and living in the power of the Holy Spirit.

When the battle feels overwhelming, remember that "thanks be to God, who delivers me through Jesus Christ our Lord!" (Romans 7:25). Victory is already ours in Christ, and through Him, we can overcome the battle with self and fulfill our God-given purpose.

Chapter 11: Finding Purpose in Pain

Pain is an inevitable part of the human experience. Whether it is physical suffering, emotional heartache, or spiritual anguish, pain can be a deeply unsettling force. Yet, for those who are in Christ, pain is never meaningless. It is often through our pain that God works in the deepest parts of our hearts, refining us, shaping us, and drawing us closer to Him. In this chapter, we will explore how pain can become a tool for growth and spiritual refinement, how we can trust God's sovereignty even in our suffering, and how God has a greater purpose for us through the trials we face.

—-

Pain as a Tool for Growth and Spiritual Refinement

God does not cause pain for the sake of pain, but He uses it as a tool to refine us and make us more like Christ. James 1:2-4 reminds us: "Consider it pure joy, my brothers and sisters, whenever you face trials of many kinds, because you know that the testing of your faith produces perseverance. Let perseverance finish its work so that you may be mature and complete, not lacking anything." This perspective is revolutionary because it shifts the focus of pain from mere suffering to spiritual growth.

1. Pain Produces Perseverance

In the midst of pain, it is easy to want to give up. But the Bible encourages us to view trials as opportunities for growth. Pain tests our faith, and through that testing, we are strengthened. Just as muscles grow stronger when subjected to resistance, our faith grows stronger through trials.

Practical Application: When you experience pain, ask God to help you view it as an opportunity to grow in perseverance. Rather than focusing on the pain, focus on how you can grow through it—how you can trust God more deeply and learn His lessons in the midst of difficulty.

2. Pain Refines Our Character

Romans 5:3-4 tells us: "We also glory in our sufferings, because we know that suffering produces perseverance; perseverance, character; and character, hope." Pain does not just build perseverance; it refines our character. It reveals areas of weakness and dependence on self, and through that, it allows God to mold us into His image.

Practical Application: When facing pain, ask yourself, "What is God trying to teach me through this?" Seek to grow in humility, patience, and dependence on God. Allow the experience to refine your character, making you more like Christ.

3. Pain Helps Us Depend on God

In our suffering, we are often reminded of our inability to handle things on our own. Pain forces us to rely on God in ways that comfort and ease do not. It is in the moments of deepest anguish that we find ourselves reaching out to God, seeking His strength and guidance.

Practical Application: Use times of pain to deepen your dependence on God. Turn to Him in prayer, seek His word for comfort, and trust in His provision, knowing that He is near to the brokenhearted (Psalm 34:18).

—-

The Story of Joseph: From Betrayal to Fulfilling God's Purpose

One of the most powerful examples of finding purpose in pain is the story of Joseph. Joseph's life was marked by betrayal, injustice, and suffering. Yet, through it all, he remained faithful to God, and God ultimately used his pain to bring about His greater purpose.

1. Joseph's Betrayal

Joseph's brothers, out of jealousy and hatred, sold him into slavery (Genesis 37). He was taken to Egypt, far from his family, and faced years of hardship and injustice. He was falsely accused of a crime he did not commit, and as a result, he was thrown into prison (Genesis 39). At every turn, it seemed as though Joseph's life was spiraling into hopelessness.

Practical Application: When you face betrayal or injustice, remember Joseph's story. Even when others hurt you or misunderstand you, trust that God sees your pain and that He is working behind the scenes for your good.

2. Joseph's Faithfulness in Adversity

Despite the betrayal and hardship, Joseph did not turn away from God. In every circumstance, whether as a slave or a prisoner, Joseph continued to honor God with his actions and decisions. His faithfulness did not go unnoticed, and he was eventually promoted to a high position in Pharaoh's court.

Practical Application: In the midst of your pain, choose to remain faithful to God. Honor Him with your actions, even when it feels difficult, trusting that He is with you through every trial.

3. Joseph's Redemption and Purpose Fulfilled

In the end, Joseph's suffering was not in vain. When a famine struck the land, Joseph's brothers came to Egypt seeking food. They did not recognize Joseph, but Joseph recognized them. Instead of seeking revenge, Joseph forgave them, understanding that all that had happened was part of God's plan. In Genesis 50:20, Joseph says to his brothers: "You intended to harm me, but God intended it for good to accomplish what is now being done, the saving of many lives." What seemed like a series of painful, unjust events was actually God's providence at work.

Practical Application: When you experience pain, remember that God's purposes are often larger than our understanding. Trust that He is working all things together for good, even when it's hard to see. Look for His hand in the midst of your suffering, knowing that He will use it to fulfill His purposes.

—-

Learning to Trust God's Sovereignty Even in Suffering

The key to finding purpose in pain is learning to trust God's sovereignty. God is not distant or indifferent to our suffering; rather, He is fully aware of it, and He has a plan. Trusting in His sovereignty means believing that He is in control of every situation, even when it doesn't make sense.

1. God's Sovereignty Over Our Lives

God's sovereignty means that He rules over all things, including our pain. Psalm 115:3 declares: "Our God is in heaven; He does whatever pleases Him." This includes allowing us to walk through seasons of difficulty. While pain is not enjoyable, it is never outside of God's control. He allows it for reasons beyond our comprehension, but He always works it for His glory and our good.

Practical Application: In times of suffering, remind yourself that God is in control. Even when you don't understand the why, trust that He is faithful and that He will bring you through.

2. Trusting God's Timing

In our pain, we often want immediate relief. But God's timing is perfect. Isaiah 55:8-9 reminds us: "For my thoughts are not your thoughts, neither are your ways my ways," declares the Lord. "As the heavens are higher than the earth, so are my ways higher than your ways and my thoughts than your thoughts." God's purpose in our pain may not be immediately apparent, but we can trust that His timing is always for our good and His glory.

Practical Application: When you are in pain, ask God for patience and trust in His timing. Remember that He is working even when you can't see it. Hold on to the promise that He is making all things beautiful in His time (Ecclesiastes 3:11).

3. Learning to Rest in God's Sovereignty

Resting in God's sovereignty means accepting that He has a purpose for our pain, even when it is difficult to understand. Jesus Himself walked the path of suffering, knowing that it was necessary to fulfill God's plan of redemption. Hebrews 12:2 tells us that "For the joy set before Him, He endured the cross, scorning its shame." Jesus trusted that His suffering would bring about the salvation of the world, and we can trust that our suffering is not in vain.

Practical Application: Rest in the assurance that God is sovereign over all things, including your pain. Surrender your suffering to Him, knowing that He is using it for a greater purpose that will ultimately bring Him glory.

—-

Conclusion: Purpose Found in Pain

Pain is not meaningless; it is an opportunity for growth, refinement, and a deeper trust in God's sovereignty. Through the story of Joseph, we see that God can take even the most painful circumstances and turn them into something beautiful. By learning to trust in God's greater purpose, we can find hope and purpose even in the midst of suffering.

No matter what pain you are facing today, remember that God is with you, He is working in you, and He will use your pain for His glory. Trust in His sovereign plan, and know that your suffering is never in vain when it is surrendered to Him.

Chapter 12: Living with Eternal Perspective

Life on earth is brief, a vapor that vanishes quickly. In the grand scheme of eternity, the struggles and successes we experience may seem small, yet they are significant when viewed in the light of God's greater purpose for our lives. Living with an eternal perspective means understanding that our actions, choices, and relationships on earth have lasting implications. This perspective shifts how we view everything—our suffering, our joys, and our ambitions. In this chapter, we will explore the fleeting nature of earthly life, the importance of storing treasures in heaven, and how viewing our challenges and successes through the lens of eternity transforms how we live.

The Fleeting Nature of Earthly Life

James 4:14 reminds us of the brevity of life: "Why, you do not even know what will happen tomorrow. What is your life? You are a mist that appears for a little while and then vanishes." Life on earth is incredibly short. While we may experience years of joy or suffering, the time we have here pales in comparison to eternity.

1. Life as a Vapor

James uses the imagery of a vapor or mist to describe life. Just as a mist appears briefly and then disappears, so too is our earthly life. The time we have is limited, and we are not guaranteed another moment. This should not cause fear, but it should give us a sense of urgency to live wisely and with purpose.

Practical Application: Reflect daily on the fleeting nature of life. Let this awareness motivate you to live intentionally, prioritizing what truly matters—your relationship with God, your love for others, and the way you contribute to His kingdom.

2. The Call to Eternal Significance

When we understand that life is short, we begin to realize that it is the eternal things that matter most. Our relationship with God, the love we show others, and the way we live according to His will are the only things that will last beyond this world. Ecclesiastes 3:11 speaks of God setting eternity in our hearts, helping us to recognize that there is something beyond this temporary world—a reality that should shape how we live today.

Practical Application: Let the fleeting nature of life remind you that your time here is precious. Invest in the things that will endure, such as your relationship with God, the lives you impact, and the eternal truths of Scripture.

—-

Storing Treasures in Heaven

In Matthew 6:19-21, Jesus teaches us where to focus our efforts: "Do not store up for yourselves treasures on earth, where moths and vermin destroy, and where thieves break in and steal. But store up for yourselves treasures in heaven, where moths and vermin do not destroy, and where thieves do not break in and steal. For where your treasure is, there your heart will be also."

1. The Futility of Earthly Treasures

Earthly treasures are temporary. Material possessions, wealth, and achievements are all subject to decay, loss, or theft. The things we often spend so much of our time and energy pursuing are here today and gone tomorrow. Yet, Jesus calls us to focus on treasures in heaven—eternal rewards that can never be taken away.

Practical Application: Shift your focus from accumulating material wealth or success to investing in eternal things. How can you use your resources—time, talents, and money—to further God's kingdom and bless others? Live with the understanding that what you do for Christ is what will last forever.

2. Storing Treasures in Heaven

Treasures in heaven are not material possessions, but rather the eternal rewards that come from living a life aligned with God's will. These treasures are found in acts of love, obedience, and service to God and others. Matthew 25:21 records the words of the master: "Well done, good and faithful servant! You have been faithful with a few things; I will put you in charge of many things. Come and share your master's happiness." Our faithful service to God—whether seen by others or not—has eternal value.

Practical Application: Consider how you can store up treasures in heaven. How can you serve others, live with integrity, share the gospel, and pursue holiness? Each act of obedience and love contributes to your eternal reward.

3. Where Your Treasure Is, There Your Heart Will Be Also

Jesus' words in Matthew 6:21 are a reminder that what we treasure most reveals where our hearts are. If we treasure earthly things above all, our hearts will be consumed with those things. But if we treasure the things of God—His Word, His people, and His kingdom—our hearts will be aligned with His purposes.

Practical Application: Take time to reflect on where your heart is. What do you treasure most? Are there areas of your life where you are too focused on earthly pursuits? Seek to realign your heart with the eternal values that matter to God.

—-

Viewing Challenges and Successes in Light of Eternity

Life's challenges and successes can often be overwhelming when viewed in isolation. However, when we view them through the lens of eternity, we can see them for what they truly are—opportunities to grow, serve, and prepare for what is to come.

1. Challenges as Opportunities for Growth

In 2 Corinthians 4:17-18, Paul writes: "For our light and momentary troubles are achieving for us an eternal glory that far outweighs them all. So we fix our eyes not on what is seen, but on what is unseen, since what is seen is temporary, but what is unseen is eternal." The challenges we face, though painful, are temporary and are producing something far greater than we can imagine—eternal glory.

Practical Application: When facing difficulties, remind yourself of the eternal perspective. Ask God to use your trials to refine your character, increase your faith, and draw you closer to Him. Trust that your pain is not in vain—it is part of God's eternal plan for you.

2. Successes as Opportunities for Stewardship

Success in this life can also be viewed in light of eternity. When we achieve something—whether it's a career milestone, personal growth, or a moment of joy—we must remember that these successes are gifts from God and should be used for His glory. Our success is not to be an end in itself but a platform to serve others and further God's kingdom.

Practical Application: Use your successes to serve God and others. Whether it's your wealth, position, or influence, remember that everything you have is a gift from God. Ask yourself how you can use your success to advance the gospel and build His kingdom on earth.

3. Living with the End in Mind

An eternal perspective helps us live with the end in mind. Revelation 21:1-4 describes the new heaven and new earth where God will wipe away every tear, and there will be no more pain or suffering. When we fix our eyes on this promise, the challenges of today seem smaller in comparison. We begin to live with the anticipation of the ultimate fulfillment of God's promises.

Practical Application: Keep the eternal prize before you. Whether you are facing success or failure, remember that your ultimate reward is not of this world. Live each day with the knowledge that your labor is not in vain when done for Christ.

—-

Conclusion: Living with an Eternal Perspective

Living with an eternal perspective transforms how we view our lives. It shifts our priorities, motivates us to live intentionally, and empowers us to endure through life's challenges. When we understand the fleeting nature of earthly life and the lasting significance of our choices, we are better equipped to store up treasures in heaven and view our experiences through the lens of eternity.

As we live for God's glory, we can rest assured that every trial and success has a purpose that extends beyond this life. Let this eternal perspective guide you as you navigate the ups and downs of life, always keeping your eyes fixed on the reward that awaits you in the presence of God forever.

Chapter 13: The Power of Faith and Hope

Faith and hope are two of the most powerful forces in the Christian life. They act as anchors for our souls, providing stability and purpose even amidst life's most difficult trials. While the world offers temporary fixes for pain and uncertainty, faith and hope point us toward an eternal perspective, giving us the strength to endure and the confidence to live out God's calling. In this chapter, we will explore how faith serves as the anchor of our lives, how hope sustains us through life's uncertainties, and how we can build a lifestyle of trust in God's promises.

—-

Faith as the Anchor of Life

Hebrews 11:1 defines faith as "the substance of things hoped for, the evidence of things not seen." Faith is not wishful thinking or blind optimism. It is the confident assurance in the promises of God, even when we cannot see or understand the outcome. Faith is a choice to trust in God's character, His plan, and His power to accomplish His will in our lives. It is the foundation on which we stand when everything else in life seems unstable.

1. Faith as Trust in God's Character

At its core, faith is a deep trust in the nature of God. The Bible reveals that God is faithful, unchanging, and sovereign. Because of who He is, we can have confidence that His promises are true, even when our circumstances suggest otherwise. Hebrews 10:23 encourages us: "Let us hold unswervingly to the hope we profess, for he who promised is faithful."

Practical Application: In moments of uncertainty or difficulty, reflect on God's character. Rehearse His faithfulness in the past and remind yourself that He has never failed. Anchor your trust in the truth of who God is, not in what you see or feel in the moment.

2. Faith as Confidence in God's Promises

Faith is also the assurance that what God has promised will come to pass. Romans 4:20-21 speaks of Abraham, who "did not waver through unbelief regarding the promise of God, but was strengthened in his faith and gave glory to God, being fully persuaded that God had power to do what He had promised." Abraham's faith was not based on what he saw; it was rooted in God's trustworthiness.

Practical Application: Build your faith by meditating on God's promises in Scripture. Take time each day to remind yourself of His word and what He has assured you. Trust that His plans for you are good, and He will fulfill His promises, regardless of what your current circumstances suggest.

3. Faith as the Foundation for Action

Faith is not passive. It is the driving force behind our actions. James 2:17 tells us: "In the same way, faith by itself, if it is not accompanied by action, is dead." Faith calls us to step out and live in obedience to God's will, trusting that He will provide and guide us. It gives us the courage to act even when the outcome is uncertain.

Practical Application: Allow your faith to lead you to action. Ask God to reveal the areas in your life where you need to step out in obedience, even when it feels risky. Trust that He will honor your faith and guide your steps.

—

How Hope Sustains Us Through Life's Uncertainties

Hope is closely tied to faith, yet it carries a unique power to sustain us through life's uncertainties. Hope is the confident expectation that God's promises will come to fruition, both in this life and in the life to come. It is the light that guides us through dark valleys, the strength we need when life's storms threaten to overwhelm us.

1. Hope in the Midst of Trials

James 1:2-4 encourages us to consider it joy when we face trials, knowing that these trials test our faith and produce perseverance. Hope does not promise a life free from pain, but it promises that our pain is not in vain. Romans 5:3-5 reminds us: "We also glory in our sufferings, because we know that suffering produces perseverance; perseverance, character; and character, hope. And hope does not put us to shame, because God's love has been poured out into our hearts through the Holy Spirit, who has been given to us."

Practical Application: In times of suffering, hold on to the hope of what God is doing in you through the trial. Trust that He is refining your character and building endurance that will ultimately bring glory to Him. Let your hope in God's love and faithfulness sustain you, knowing that He is working even in the most difficult moments.

2. Hope for the Future

Hope looks not only to the present but also to the future—specifically to the promise of eternal life with God. 1 Peter 1:3-4 tells us that "In his great mercy he has given us new birth into a living hope through the resurrection of Jesus Christ from the dead, and into an inheritance that can never perish, spoil or fade." The hope we have in Christ is anchored in the certainty of eternal life, where there will be no more pain, suffering, or death. This eternal hope gives us the perspective to endure hardships in this life.

Practical Application: In times of uncertainty or discouragement, lift your eyes to the future hope that you have in Christ. Meditate on the promises of eternal life, where everything will be made right. Let this hope inspire you to persevere and live with joy, knowing that your ultimate reward is secure in Christ.

3. Hope in God's Timing

Hope is not just about the future; it also involves trusting in God's timing. In Psalm 27:14, David encourages us to "Wait for the Lord; be strong and take heart and wait for the Lord." Waiting on God can be challenging, especially when we want immediate answers or solutions. But hope enables us to trust that God's timing is perfect, and He will provide for us at the right moment.

Practical Application: Practice waiting on God with hope. Trust that He knows what you need and when you need it. Rather than rushing ahead or trying to control the outcome, surrender your desires to Him and rest in His perfect timing.

—-

Building a Lifestyle of Trust in God's Promises

Faith and hope are not just abstract concepts; they are meant to shape our daily lives. By cultivating a lifestyle of trust in God's promises, we can experience the peace and strength that come from knowing that He is faithful.

1. Daily Surrender and Trust

Building a lifestyle of trust starts with daily surrender. Each day, we must choose to trust God with our lives, our decisions, and our circumstances. Proverbs 3:5-6 urges us to "Trust in the Lord with all your heart and lean not on your own understanding; in all your ways submit to him, and he will make your paths straight." Trusting God means acknowledging that we do not have all the answers, but He does.

Practical Application: Begin each day by surrendering your plans and desires to God. Pray for His guidance, and trust that He will direct your steps. Let go of the need to control everything and allow God to take the lead.

2. Regular Meditation on God's Promises

Faith and hope grow when we immerse ourselves in God's Word. Romans 10:17 tells us: "Consequently, faith comes from hearing the message, and the message is heard through the word about Christ." Regularly meditating on God's promises strengthens our faith and reminds us of the hope we have in Him.

Practical Application: Make Scripture a daily part of your life. Read God's Word, memorize His promises, and speak them over your life. Let His truth become the foundation for your faith and the source of your hope.

3. Living Out Your Faith and Hope

Faith and hope are not only internal convictions; they should be lived out through our actions. Let your trust in God influence the way you interact with others, the way you respond to challenges, and the way you live out your purpose. Faith and hope give us the courage to step out, to love others, and to serve with joy, knowing that God is at work in us and through us.

Practical Application: Live out your faith by serving others, speaking hope into the lives of those around you, and remaining steadfast in your trust in God's promises. Let your actions reflect the faith and hope that anchor your soul.

—-

Conclusion: The Power of Faith and Hope

Faith and hope are the bedrock of the Christian life. They sustain us through life's uncertainties, anchor us in God's truth, and empower us to live out our purpose. As we trust in God's character, His promises, and His timing, we can face the challenges of life with confidence, knowing that He is faithful and that our hope is secure in Him.

Let faith be the anchor that holds you firm in the storms of life, and let hope be the light that guides you toward God's eternal promises. Build your life on these powerful gifts, and experience the peace and joy that come from living in trust and expectation of all that God has prepared for you.

Chapter 14: Walking in God's Purpose Daily

Living a purpose-driven life is not about waiting for extraordinary moments to find fulfillment; it's about faithfully walking in God's calling every day. Our lives are meant to reflect His glory in both big and small ways, and we have the privilege of living with purpose each day through our relationship with Him. In this chapter, we will explore practical steps to walk in God's purpose daily—through prayer, study of Scripture, and acts of service—and find encouragement to stay consistent despite the challenges we face.

—-

Practical Steps to Live a Purpose-Driven Life

Walking in God's purpose begins with intentionality. It's easy to become distracted by the busyness of life or the pull of worldly desires, but the Bible reminds us that we are not created to live aimlessly. As we seek God's guidance daily, we align ourselves with His will, living with the assurance that each day matters in His plan. To walk in God's purpose, we must commit ourselves to certain daily practices that keep us grounded in Him.

1. Prayer – Cultivating an Ongoing Relationship with God

Prayer is the most important practice for living a purpose-driven life. It is through prayer that we connect with God, align our hearts with His, and receive the guidance we need to fulfill His will. Jesus Himself modeled a life of prayer, seeking the Father's will at every step. In Matthew 6:10, He taught us to pray, "Your kingdom come, Your will be done on earth as it is in heaven."

Practical Application: Start your day with prayer, surrendering your plans and desires to God. Ask Him to guide you in the decisions you make, to give you wisdom for the tasks ahead, and to use you to bring glory to His name. Throughout the day, continue to engage in conversation with Him, listening for His voice and offering gratitude for His presence. Prayer is not a one-time event but an ongoing dialogue with God that keeps us connected to our purpose.

2. Study of Scripture – Renewing Your Mind Daily

The Bible is our guidebook for life. It reveals God's will, equips us for good works, and transforms our hearts and minds. Romans 12:2 reminds us to "not conform to the pattern of this world, but be transformed by the renewing of your mind." As we immerse ourselves in God's Word, our thinking aligns with His truth, and our actions reflect His character.

Practical Application: Make Bible reading a daily habit. Begin each day by meditating on Scripture, allowing it to shape your thoughts and decisions. Reflect on passages that speak to your current situation and ask the Holy Spirit to reveal deeper truths. When you face challenges, turn to God's Word for encouragement and guidance, trusting that His promises will direct your steps.

3. Acts of Service – Living Out Your Purpose Through Others

Living a purpose-driven life involves serving others. Jesus came not to be served but to serve, and He calls us to do the same (Mark 10:45). Service is a natural outflow of a heart aligned with God's purpose, and it is through serving others that we make a tangible difference in the world around us. Whether in our families, workplaces, or communities, we are called to reflect God's love and grace through our actions.

Practical Application: Look for opportunities to serve others each day, whether through a kind word, an act of generosity, or lending a helping hand. Service does not always have to be grand or public; often, the small, everyday acts of kindness reflect God's love most powerfully. By serving others, we fulfill our purpose and participate in God's work on earth.

—-

Staying Consistent Despite Challenges

Living a purpose-driven life is not without its difficulties. Life's challenges—whether personal struggles, disappointments, or external obstacles—can often make it feel as though our purpose is unclear or out of reach. However, the Bible teaches us to stay consistent in our pursuit of God's will, trusting that He is faithful to complete the work He has begun in us (Philippians 1:6).

1. Persevering Through Difficulties

When life gets difficult, it can be easy to lose sight of our purpose. Yet, God's Word encourages us to persevere, knowing that our struggles produce endurance and strengthen our faith. James 1:2-4 says, "Consider it pure joy whenever you face trials of many kinds, because you know that the testing of your faith produces perseverance. Let perseverance finish its work so that you may be mature and complete, not lacking anything."

Practical Application: When facing trials, remind yourself that your purpose is not dependent on your circumstances but on your relationship with God. Press into Him through prayer and Scripture, trusting that He is using even the difficulties for your growth and His glory. Let perseverance become a foundation for your consistency in walking out God's purpose.

2. Staying Rooted in God's Promises

Consistency is not about willpower; it's about relying on God's strength. When we face discouragement or weariness, it's easy to give up or take a break from pursuing our purpose. But when we are rooted in God's promises, we can endure. Isaiah 40:31 reminds us that "those who hope in the Lord will renew their strength. They will soar on wings like eagles; they will run and not grow weary, they will walk and not be faint."

Practical Application: When you feel tired or disheartened, take time to remember and declare God's promises over your life. Let His truth remind you of your identity and purpose. Trust that He will renew your strength as you stay rooted in His Word and continue to walk in faith.

3. Finding Encouragement in Community

One of the greatest gifts God has given us to help us walk in purpose is the body of Christ—our fellow believers. Community provides support, encouragement, and accountability as we seek to live out God's calling. Hebrews 10:24-25 urges us to "consider how we may spur one another on toward love and good deeds, not giving up meeting together, as some are in the habit of doing, but encouraging one another."

Practical Application: Be intentional about building relationships with other believers who will encourage and challenge you. Join a church group, participate in a Bible study, or seek out a mentor who can guide you in living a purpose-driven life. Surround yourself with others who are walking the same journey, and let their strength and wisdom help you stay consistent in your own walk with God.

—-

Conclusion: Walking in God's Purpose Every Day

Living a purpose-driven life is not just a one-time decision; it's a daily commitment to prayer, Scripture study, and acts of service. It's a lifestyle of intentionality, where each day becomes an opportunity to walk in God's purpose. Although challenges may come, we are reminded that consistency is key, and our faithfulness to God will bear fruit in His time.

As you walk in God's purpose daily, remember that He is with you every step of the way. Let prayer anchor you, let Scripture guide you, and let acts of service reflect God's love to the world. Stay rooted in His promises, persevere through trials, and lean on the support of your community. In doing so, you will live a life that glorifies God and fulfills the purpose He has set before you.

Chapter 15: Conclusion – The Fulfilled Life

As we come to the end of this journey through the purpose of life, we revisit the key themes that have guided our exploration: joy, sadness, relationships, and eternal purpose. These elements are intertwined in the tapestry of life, each playing a unique role in shaping our understanding of what it means to live purposefully. The ultimate fulfillment of life is not found in worldly achievements or temporary pleasures, but in a life that is rooted in Christ—our Savior, Redeemer, and the source of all true joy and meaning. In this final chapter, we reflect on the journey we have undertaken and call each of us to embrace God's purpose with faith, courage, and commitment.

—-

Revisiting the Key Themes

1. Joy

We began by exploring joy as a fruit of the Spirit—a joy that transcends circumstances and is deeply rooted in our relationship with God. Joy is not about fleeting happiness or external achievements, but about knowing and delighting in the presence of our Creator. In Christ, we find the source of joy that sustains us through every season of life. Joy is found in His love, His grace, and His unchanging goodness.

Reflection: Take time to consider how you can cultivate joy in your daily life. Reflect on the goodness of God, His faithfulness, and His promises, allowing joy to overflow from your heart in both the easy and difficult moments.

2. Sadness

Sadness is a natural part of the human experience, yet it does not have the final word in our lives. Through biblical examples like Job and David, we saw how God meets us in our sorrow and uses it to refine us, strengthen our faith, and draw us closer to Him. The promise of Psalm 34:18 reminds us, "The Lord is close to the brokenhearted and saves those who are crushed in spirit." Sadness does not diminish our purpose; it deepens our reliance on God and opens our hearts to His comfort and healing.

Reflection: When facing sadness, let it be a moment to lean more fully on God. Trust that even in sorrow, God is at work, refining your character and preparing you for greater purposes ahead.

3. Relationships

Our relationships with others are not only reflections of God's love but also a key part of our purpose. Jesus commanded us to love God and love our neighbors (Matthew 22:37-39), making relationships a central theme in God's design for our lives. In friendships, marriages, families, and communities, we experience the joy of sharing life with others, growing together in faith, and holding each other accountable in our pursuit of God's will.

Reflection: Evaluate your relationships and ask God to help you cultivate love, grace, and mutual encouragement. Seek out opportunities to serve others, to be a light in the lives of those around you, and to strengthen the bonds that reflect God's love to the world.

4. Eternal Purpose

The ultimate purpose of life is to glorify God and enjoy Him forever. Our time on earth is fleeting, but the impact of living in alignment with God's eternal purposes carries on for eternity. In the context of eternity, our struggles, achievements, and sacrifices find their true meaning. As we store up treasures in heaven (Matthew 6:19-21), we are reminded that the fulfillment we seek in this life is found in living for God's glory and not our own.

Reflection: Remind yourself daily of the eternal significance of your actions. Live with an eternal perspective, where your decisions, work, and relationships are guided by the purpose of glorifying God and advancing His kingdom.

—-

The Fulfilled Life is Found in Christ

John 10:10 presents the heart of the gospel: "I have come that they may have life, and have it to the full." Jesus offers a life of abundance—not in material wealth or worldly success, but in the deep, transformative fulfillment that comes from knowing Him. The fulfilled life is not about the absence of difficulty but the presence of God in every circumstance. It's about walking in the purpose He has designed for you, finding joy in His presence, and trusting that every part of your life is woven into His eternal plan.

The fulfilled life is a life of relationship with Jesus, where He is both Savior and Lord. As we align ourselves with His purpose, we experience true freedom—freedom to live, to love, and to serve according to the will of God. In Christ, we find the fulfillment we were created for, and in Him, all of life's pieces—joy, sorrow, relationships, and purpose—find their proper place.

Reflection: Ask yourself: Is your life being lived in pursuit of the fullness that Christ offers? Are you allowing Him to guide you, fulfill you, and lead you into His purpose each day?

—-

A Final Call to Embrace God's Purpose

As you close this book, I invite you to step into the life God has designed for you. Embrace His purpose with faith and courage. Trust that He has uniquely created you with gifts, talents, and a calling that are part of His grand plan. It may not always be easy, and there will be challenges along the way, but remember that you are never alone. God walks with you, guiding you, strengthening you, and empowering you to live a life of significance and eternal impact.

Embrace your calling to glorify God, to love others, and to live in the fullness of life that Jesus offers. The purpose of life is not something you need to search for from the outside—it's found in walking daily with Christ and allowing His will to shape your steps. The journey will not be without difficulty, but it will be one of joy, purpose, and eternal significance.

—-

Conclusion: A Life Well-Lived

In the end, a fulfilled life is one that is lived in alignment with God's purpose. It's a life marked by deep joy, even in the midst of sadness, a life shaped by relationships that reflect His love, and a life focused on an eternal purpose. The promise of Jesus is that when we live for Him, we will find life—not just any life, but life to the full.

May you walk boldly in God's purpose for your life, knowing that He has called you, equipped you, and empowered you to live in the fullness of His love and grace.

Tawanda Tawanda

[skiesonlinemedia@gmail.com]

Don't miss out!

Visit the website below and you can sign up to receive emails whenever Tawanda Tawanda publishes a new book. There's no charge and no obligation.

https://books2read.com/r/B-A-JMDYC-RHFLF

BOOKS 2 READ

Connecting independent readers to independent writers.

Also by Tawanda Tawanda

Life After Divorce
African Child
Purpose of Life

www.ingramcontent.com/pod-product-compliance
Lightning Source LLC
LaVergne TN
LVHW091122150826
845673LV00002B/944
* 9 7 9 8 2 3 0 8 0 6 9 8 1 *